THE ART OF WAITING

NEWTON DUAH YEBOAH

ISBN 979-8-89112-497-4 (Paperback)
ISBN 979-8-89112-498-1 (Digital)

Covenant Books
11661 Hwy 707
Murrells Inlet, SC 29576
www.covenantbooks.com

To God Almighty. He gave me the inspiration and the zeal to write this book. In Him I live and have my being. Oh, God, I love you because you first loved me.

Contents

Foreword

The vision is yet for an appointed time but at the end it shall speak and not lie. Though it tarries, wait for it because it will surely come. (Habakkuk 2:3)

Until the time his word came true, the word of the Lord tried him. That was Joseph. (Psalm 105:19)

If you faint in the day of adversity, thy strength is small. (Proverbs 24:10)

In between the word *prophecy* and its fulfillment is called the maturity time. What many people do not understand is that the waiting period is the training school of the Holy Spirit. For how long you remain in this period is totally up to you. As soon as you learn the lesson the Holy Spirit is trying to teach you, you are promoted.

But many people do not know what to do in their waiting time, therefore they fall prey to the devil. This masterpiece is timely and challenging. I therefore endorse this book for you to know the keys to your survival in the time of your waiting until the time of visitation.

Bishop Professor Stephen Owusu Jackson
Chairman of Christian Praise
International Centre (CPIC)
Accra, Ghana

Second Foreword

Just as a farmer has to wait for the seed sown to grow and mature and bear fruits, so do we have to wait for the fulfillment of God's promises in our lives. Our problem is waiting for the fulfillment of the promises made by God.

Several challenges crop up, which sometimes, if care is not taken, divert our focus from the delivery of the promises. Some of us give up within this period and eventually lose faith in the ability and the faithfulness of God. The devil then takes advantage of our impatience and lack of endurance and manipulates us into submission.

The writer of this book has come out with some divine solutions to the challenges that we normally encounter while waiting for the fulfillment of God's promises in our lives. I recommend that you read this book and arm yourself with such divine tools that are designed to help you overcome possible challenges in the period of waiting so that you can celebrate the faithfulness of God in your life.

Remember, once He has promised, surely, he will do. Hold on to your faith and arm yourself with the tools of overcoming challenges in waiting so that God's name will be glorified in your life. Welcome on board as we navigate the scriptures for such tools for overcoming the challenges that crop up during our waiting periods.

Apostle Moses Boahen, General Secretary
Christian Praise International Centre Tema
Accra, Ghana

Preface

This book came about when I was in great pain and anguish. There was no hope for me in life. The inspiration from the Lord came to me in my time of seclusion and destitute.

I was the cost controller of a three-star hotel that was about to be migrated to a four-star hotel. By then it was the best hotel in Tema, Ghana, the main harbor city of Ghana in West Africa. Life was very good. I had a piggery farm and another land I had intended to use for a poultry farm. My CEO liked me so much. Most of the time, in the absence of a general manager, she entrusts the running of the entire hotel to my care. When she leaves Ghana to visit the USA, she does not communicate with any of the managers but me. Any information must go through me to reach her. At a point in time, I was like her favorite employee. She promoted me to be the financial controller of the hotel which I honestly did not like for some personal reasons.

She never had a problem with me. Just a week after the promotion letter from the cost controller to become the financial controller, she asked the human resource manager to serve me a letter to proceed on indefinite leave with half pay for three months. I called her on the phone and asked what I did wrong, but it seemed like she did not know why she wanted me to go on indefinite leave. It appeared like I had not done anything wrong, but she just wanted me to go, and she did not even know why.

I decided to give her some time, hoping that I would get my half salary and would be called back to work, but nothing. No half pay, and I was not called back after five months. Apparently, she called IT experts to check my computer if I had done something wrong, but they found nothing on my computer. I started demanding for my salary. My salary for the month I was asked to go home was not paid also. Later I received a letter that I had been sacked because I was corrupt.

I took the case to the labor office in Tema for them to come and explain why they said I was corrupt and they were refusing to give me my salary and other entitlements. I needed them to come to the labor office with their facts that I was corrupt because ACCA, the accounting body in which I work in their name, would not allow me to practice accounting in their name if I was corrupt. (NB: I was not a charted accountant, but I had done parts 1 and 2 of the ACCA course.)

Their representative came to the labor office, and they had no basis for the corrupt accusation, so they were compelled to pay my salary and my provident fund, which they paid, although they cheated me.

I invested all my money in my piggery farm and corn farming on my land. My intention was to cultivate corn and store with the hope of cutting down feeding costs when I start my poultry farm. My land is situated in a rainfall zone. In the season in which I cultivated, there was no rain, and not even a single stick of corn about nine acres survived. My piggery farm became a huge loss. Most died, and the person I hired to take care of the pigs sold most without my knowledge. The farm was far away from me, and I could not visit there often for lack of money.

I eventually lost everything. My job was gone. The only investment I had just went down the drain. I did not have even a cent in my pocket or bank account. I could not take care of my home. The scripture that came to my mind was Habakkuk 3:17: "Although the fig tree shall not blossom, neither shall fruits be in the vines; the labor of the olive shall fail and the fields shall yield no meat; the flock shall be cut off from the fold. And there shall be no heard be in the stalls; yet I will rejoice in the Lord. I will joy in the God of my salvation." Even in this confession, I was crying like a baby in prayer.

One night, in my sorrowful time of prayer and tears, I heard in my spirit that this was my waiting period. If only I am able to go through it, I will be greater than before. From that very moment, I started receiving inspiration in my spirit as if a man was reading a book to console me in my spirit and I began to write. I never planned to write this book, and it never seemed to me like I was authoring a book. Apparently, I had tried to author a book years ago, but after putting together a manuscript of fourteen chapters, I threw it somewhere that I never looked for. Shortly after that manuscript, I had a dream about a great man on a throne telling me that I was already blessed and this book I have authored will take me to nations and by this book I will meet people of power, influence, and wealth. It was about seven years later that this book was written.

When I finally sent my manuscript to Covenant Books Inc. in South Carolina to go through, they expressed interest in publishing the book in the USA and invited me to come to the USA. I never knew how possible I could enter the USA. It looked impossible for me to obtain a visa; but my father, Rev. Richard Oduro, told me he saw me in the USA, so I should attend the visa interview. My visa was approved, and here I am in the USA.

Part of the dream I had, which says this book, will take me to nations has started coming through and God used the USA as my starting point. At the time I had that dream, *The Art of Waiting* was not authored. It seems the Lord wanted my attention so he could give me this book to author, but I was too busy as a cost controller for a hotel, and I could not receive from him. I hardly prayed when I was a cost controller. I could not even pray for three minutes when life was good back then. But when God allowed the devil to bring me down so he could get my attention, he gave me a book to author. Now I am able to pray for hours all by myself. I was angry with my former CEO for firing me, but now I am blessing her wherever she is for sacking me. Had she not fired me, this book would not have been written. If this book had not been written, I would not have received the invitation to come to the USA. As I was told in the dream, I know that by this book and the eleven other books the Lord has given me, I will travel the world and spread his word. And with no iota of a doubt, I will meet people of power, influence, and wealth.

My brethren, be willing to go through the process and God will make the best out of you. At any moment you see yourself in any kind of problem, thank God and focus on him. It will turn for your glory.

Acknowledgments

First and foremost, I acknowledge God the Almighty, Jesus Christ, the son of the living God and the Holy Spirit, for imparting such a stupendous grace upon my life to positively affect many lives. Who am I to come before the holy ambience of His presence if not by His grace and love? I thank God for all that I am and all that I will ever be. I owe everything to Him.

Secondly, I thank my dear mother, Comfort Birago. Mum, your prayer, encouragement, love, directions, and support are taking me far. Indeed you are a gift from God to us all. Actually I was able to write the epilogue of this book due to a story you told. I am so very grateful to you, Mum.

A big thank you to my father, Rev. Richard Oduro. God used you to prophesy to me that I will be in the USA, and I am here. You prayed for my wife who was medically barren for almost ten years, and she is pregnant and about to deliver. By my encounter with you, I have become a new man inside out and deeply rooted in the word of God now and more prayerful than ever. God bless you for me, sir.

To my empress, Mrs. Linda Newton Duah Yeboah, I thank you so much for believing in me. Your prayers, patience, support, and encouragement helped me so much. Thank you so much, my dear.

To my late stepfather, Mr. Alfred Duah, I say a big thank you. Even as I never knew my biological father, you accepted me not just as a son, but you made me your walking stick. You have been a father and a brother to myself and my siblings. God bless you, Daddy.

A very big thank you to my parents here in the USA, Mr. Rodger Carter and Mrs. Rachel Carter. God bless you for me, Mum and Dad. When I got to the USA, I had nowhere to go. You brought me into your home and made me part of your beautiful family. You clothed, sheltered, and fed me. God bless you for me. Had the Lord not brought you to me, I do not know how I would have survived in the USA. Thank you.

There was a time in my life I did not believe in the love of God. I thought God hated me. I did not like going to church. It took a great man of God to teach me the ways of God and snatched me from the traps and the destructions of the enemy. He groomed me and gave me the opportunity to be featured on our local church activities. He never gave up on me. Due to his close monitoring and advice, I could not stay away from church services as I used to. He used to sit me down in his office for hours to encourage me. He privately taught me the word of God almost every week. I am so grateful for the seed he sowed in me, and I am more grateful for him being the writer of this book's foreword. Bishop Prof. Stephen Owusu Jackson, Chairman of Christian Praise International Centre, your son says thank you so much, and may God bless you for me.

I am again grateful for the teachings, advice, and directions from my former Apostle, Moses Boahen, the General Secretary of CPIC. He taught me the principles of life and now I can stand and face life as a man. He prepared me for a better tomorrow. Under his leadership, he pushes me to do things that I thought I could never have done. If today, I can teach from the scriptures and inspire others, it is due to the good training he is taking me through. Thank you so much for being the writer of this book's second foreword. God bless you for me.

How can I forget my scriptural rabbi? He has time for me in the matters of the scriptures like no other. As a student of the Bible, I always have questions, I'm always curious, and I desire to know everything in the scriptures. When it comes to learning the scriptures and finding answers to mysteries and mind-boggling questions, I always count on you. You always spend hours with me in the scriptures whenever I come to you. Hours become like seconds when I am doing Bible exposition with you. Bishop John Nhyira Ali, the founder and the leader of Jesus Healing Unctionem Ministry, God bless you so much for being there for me all the time. Thank you for being the shoulder I lean on to cry whenever I need.

A very big thank you to my kid brother, Obed Appiah Frimpong, the CEO of Phoenix Graphix. God bless you for me for all that you did for me. You have played a very vital role in making this book a success. I thank you for your time to design and to print this book. God bless you for me.

A very big thanks to my one and only sister, Mrs. Abigail Appiah Kusi. She has always wanted nothing but the best for us all. God bless you for your selfless sacrifices and inspirations. I will always love you.

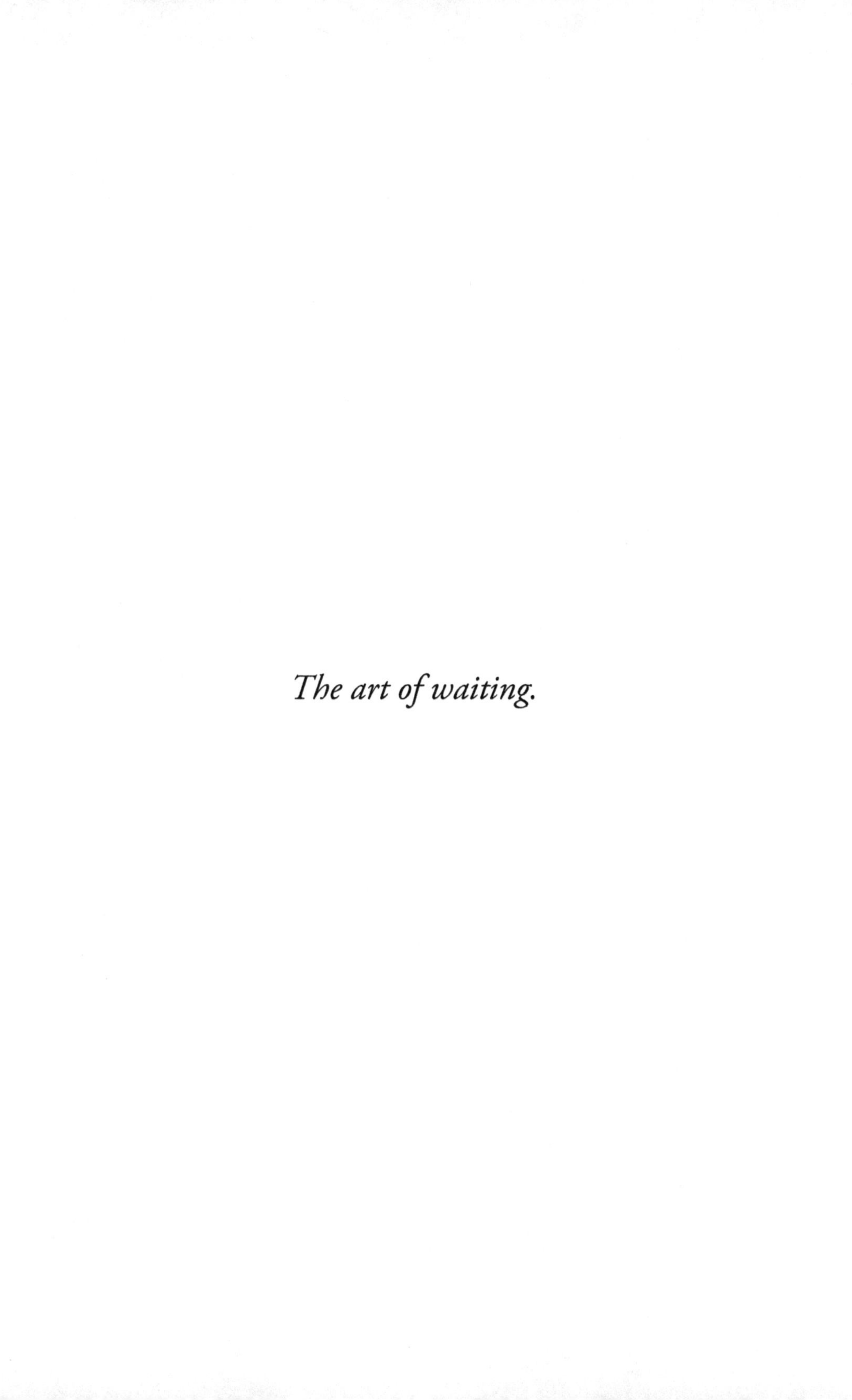

The art of waiting.

Introduction

Waiting is the act of staying where you are until a particular or an appointed time of event comes. You are in waiting for any heart's desire that you have not gotten yet. Between this moment and the time you get that special thing or attain the level you desire in life is called a waiting period. Although you are working at it, you are still waiting to get there.

No single person likes the idea of waiting. Imagine you are driving in a hurry and the traffic light shows red for you to wait for either pedestrians to cross or for other cars to take their turn to move. You begin to tap the steering wheel with your fingers in anticipation to speed off.

People are always desperate to avoid waiting periods—why? Because many lack the ability to master this great period in their lives. Among all the periods in our lives, the most crucial and challenging is the period of waiting. This period can make or unmake you. A lot of people go through tough times in their waiting periods. The tough times in the waiting period make some great, but for others, it mars their lives. The little thing you may do wrong at the moment of waiting can cost you for generations and even your generations not yet born. Waiting is not idleness in the agenda of God. Everyone is expected to do something in the period of waiting.

Waiting is accompanied by a great deal of work. It is a very trying moment that must be handled with wisdom, caution, calmness, and great effort. Waiting periods are the darkest periods in the lives of people. This period arises when one is in expectation or anxious of something, either good or bad. Somebody somewhere may be waiting for your downfall. It is good for that person, but it is bad for you.

Your waiting period may be for a financial breakthrough, but it seems you are waiting in vain. You may be waiting for marriage, but you look at yourself and you do not see any difference between you and those growing old yet no marriage. You may be looking for the fruit of the womb, but you are not getting it, yet all your mates are having children.

You may be at a crossroad waiting on God for a direction on the next step to take, but you do not hear from Him. The other day, Job said, "I sought for the Lord and I perceived Him not." Job went forward and backward, yet he could not find God in his deepest despair. He was eagerly waiting on God, but he was not getting any answer. What do you do when you are so anxious for a response in your devastating moment whereby answer is not forthcoming? Many are those that mess up in their season of waiting for lack of patience and faith in God.

Anyone that waits hangs on a promise or faith about what he or she is waiting for. Most of the time we either lose our faith or we get tired of waiting, so we choose to help ourselves. It is so easy for you to keep waiting when all things are working according to your plan. It is so easy for one to wait when he or she knows how long the waiting will last. What do you do when you do not know how long your waiting period is? Everybody will be asked to wait for one thing or the other in life before what he or she treasures will be released. Even Our Lord Jesus Christ, the Prince of Peace, was asked by God to wait at a point in his life for all his enemies to be put under his feet according to Psalms 110:1. The other day, Jesus told the disciples to wait in the upper room for the Holy Spirit to come upon them before they go out to spread the gospel.

No matter how deadly and crucial the situation might seem, the moment we are asked to wait, we just have to obey. Samuel asked King Saul to wait for him to come and offer the burnt sacrifice before he went to war. King Saul could not wait. Samuel tarried, but he did not delay. He arrived on time, but because King Saul could not deal with the challenges of waiting, Prophet Samuel told King Saul that he has acted foolishly. The dynasty was taken from his household. This is what one mess in our waiting period can do to us.

There are doom days for everyone on this earth. Life is full of surprises and uncertainties. Lives are shaped in tragedies. It does not seem like what you are going through in your waiting period is building you up, but it is actually preparing you for the best. We are often told that problems and waiting are always from the devil. I bet to differ. It is not always so. The tribulations we go through in waiting teaches us patience, faith in God, and it reveals us to ourselves. Sometimes God puts us on hold in waiting so we could have experience. David was born to become the King of Israel, but God put him on hold in the wilderness for him to gain experience of leadership via shepherding sheep. After David was anointed, the King of Israel still had to wait for years. God was building him. His greatest test, which was to fight Goliath, was in his waiting period. It was after his victory over

Goliath that the whole nation wished to have him as king.

We fight lions and bears in the waiting period. Most of us wander in the desert without water in our times of waiting. No sense of direction, no hope, and our souls thirst for the basics of life yet receive none. But those that are able to go through this process live a life of testaments.

The question is, what do you do in your darkest time? How you handle your darkest period determines how you will handle the treasure you are aspiring to get. According to a professor of the Bible, Prof. Jackson Owusu Stephen, First Chairman of Christian Praise International Centre, "Delay from God is not denial." In other words, waiting for your greatness does not mean it will never come. God's delay is for a purpose in disguise. No one would wish to receive any good thing in a premature stage. Any premature thing is fragile and can easily get destroyed when attacked.

In this book, I shall attempt to bring to light some of the ways to handle ourselves in our times of waiting. Before the manifestation of your dream, you will go through a waiting period. It is an unpleasant and lonely stage no one wishes to be. It can make you restless, agitated, very uncomfortable, missed feelings, and even so many thoughts can go to and from your mind, and at times lead you into a state of great dilemma and confusion. I refer to the waiting period as the abyss of life. In waiting, you may even wonder if what you are waiting for will ever be materialized, but I am here to encourage you that whatever you are waiting for is also waiting for you. I pray God gives you understanding and nuggets of wisdom from above to master your waiting period as you read this book.

May the Spirit of God infuse you with strength so that you will be able to deal with the challenges of waiting to birth your greatness.

Chapter 1

Patience

Patience is not about waiting but the ability to keep a good attitude while waiting.

One of the recommended antidotes to some of the challenges encountered in the period of waiting is *patience.*

Patience is the ability to accept or tolerate delays, problems, or sufferings without becoming annoyed or anxious. You may be in the most dangerous situation of your life when all are against you in your moment of waiting. Friends and family may look down upon you and make mockery of you in your time of despair. It may be loss of job and you may have to depend on people you used to help when you were working. They might have gotten tired of you as all things indicates that there is no hope to rise up again. My dear, I am here to tell you, whatever situation you find yourself in, it is not permanent. It is a phase which is passing by. If only you will persevere in patience, you will conquer. I dare you not to fear.

The story of Abraham and Sarah in the Bible better illustrates how patience can be used as a tool in mastering some of the challenges during waiting. This couple was not able to bring forth a child; all factors of having a child were against them. Abraham thought his servant Eliezer of Damascus would be his heir since he had no child of his own. God gave him a promise from his word that a son from his own body is coming, and as many are the stars of the heavens so shall his descendants be. At this moment of their lives, there was no sign that they could ever have a child. Abraham's manhood was not working, and the wife's womb was as good as dead. Yet God has given them a promise that they will give birth.

Maybe you are also in need of a child after being married for so many years. You may even be in desperate need of financial breakthrough, marriage, job, etc. The more you try, the more you fail. Sometimes, you ask yourself, why you? I am here to tell you it is not over until you win. Just have patience.

After the promise was given to Abraham, his wife got tired of waiting and suggested to Abraham to sleep with her maidservant Hagar and raise a child for her. Abraham had not gotten tired of waiting even at the point Sarah was fed up with waiting. It was hard for Abraham to accept the idea of fathering a child with Hagar. If you read the scriptures well, you will see that it took Abraham ten years before he accepted his wife's request. He was a man of faith. Perhaps he agreed to sleep with Hagar due to Sarah's constant nagging for ten years. Sarah was very desperate to the extent that she wanted to help herself. In the eyes of Sarah, all things were against her. She felt God will not do it for her. She accepted her defeat. I hereby encourage you to hold on. God has eyes and he sees your cry. He has ears and He hears your prayer. The moment, you feel in your heart so strong to give up on yourself and your case, or the moment you wish to find an alternative means to help yourself, I want you to know and bear in mind that your victory is just at the door.

Sarah could not wait for the promise to be delivered unto them. She thought God was wasting their time, but He was actually working with time and on time. Sarah rushed, and at the end, she regretted it. There is one thing I would like you to know here.

Our waiting periods are periods we prove to God that we are matured. Proving our maturity comes in diverse ways. We should be able to stand the test of time and to be approved by the divine standards of God. The time Sarah was putting pressure on Abraham to sleep with her maidservant, Hagar, God was silent. He never talked to Abraham, neither did He show him what to do.

We should not expect God to do our exams for us. He wants us to sit for our exams ourselves. Some people say they do not see God whenever they face a storm. In the middle of the storm, they need God so much, they do not see him anywhere. Bishop J. D. Jakes said in one of his teachings that we do not see clearly in the middle of storms, so we should not expect to see God in the storm. That is why the Bible tells us to walk by faith but not by sight.

We have to believe in faith that God is with us in all situations as the Bible makes us understand. If the Bible says God is with us in all situations, then it settles the matter. The Bible makes us understand that Abraham was a man of faith. He never lost faith in the abilities and the promises of God.

I am persuaded to believe that he might have agreed to sleep with Hagar due to the ten years of nagging and complaints from his wife. Perhaps, he still believed in the promise of God, but he did what he did to satisfy his wife. Whether Abraham should or should not have slept with Hagar was an exam for him. Whether he failed or passed is in the hands of God, but one thing that I know for sure is, the man had a strong faith in God. The Bible says his faith was credited to him as righteous.

What am I trying to tell you here? I want you to know that Abraham was not willing to go against the word of God. He was just waiting for the fulfilment of the promise. He had patience. Sarah could not master her waiting period with patience. At the time God gave her Isaac, she regretted for allowing her husband to father a child with her maidservant.

Let me share with you one true story my former, Apostle Moses Boahen, shared with me. This story happened at Chiraa in the Bono region of Ghana. There was a deaconess in one of the best and popular Pentecostal churches in Ghana that I do not want to mention the name. She was waiting for marriage. She loved God and her church. She was a strong pillar among the deaconesses of the church.

At one point, she became desperate and heeded to the advice of friends that she was growing old.

Apparently, several prophecies from the church leadership have been given to her to wait patiently for her marriage because the man that will marry her will come from abroad.

Finally, she gave up and renounced her faith as a Christian and became a second wife to one Muslim. She relocated to Tamale in the northern region of Ghana.

Surprisingly, there was a gentleman that was in the same church with this lady at Chiraa. He desired her for a wife. He never told the lady about his intentions, and he miraculously got an opportunity to travel to Europe.

Few days after the lady had become a second wife to a Muslim, the gentleman came to Ghana purposely to locate the lady and marry her so both can leave Ghana for Europe. Friends told him that the lady he was looking for was a second wife to one Muslim living in the northern part of Ghana. The gentleman said he will not believe until he sees the lady.

The moment the lady realized what she has missed, she cried bitterly and even wanted to divorce the Muslim husband for this gentleman. But the man said he cannot take someone's wife from him so he left.

Until you miss something, you will not see the importance of patience in waiting. Do not lose something and later say, "Had I known…" If this deaconess had held on to the tool of patience, she would not have missed such a great blessing.

We also need patience in other not to commit irreparable mistake in our waiting period. Though our desire may tarry, but it will never delay. Isaac tarried but he did not delay. He came at the right time. Do not rush to marry the wrong person. Do not be in hurry to sell your soul to the devil for riches and for fame. Just have patience in your waiting period and you will be great at the end.

Patience is bitter, but its fruit is sweet.

Chapter 2

Sacrifice

*If you don't sacrifice for what you want,
what you want will be sacrificed.*

Sacrifice is letting something of value go for the purpose of achieving a heart's desire. Anytime you give out, you receive another thing in return. If the thing you let go does not break you or cause a great vacuum in your life, the reward you receive is inevitably small. Knowingly or unknowingly, you make sacrifices in your life daily. Unfortunately, some people sacrifice the miracle they intend to wait for by a way of not sacrificing certain things.

The aim of this chapter is to introduce you to one of the powerful tools in dealing with some challenges we encounter during our waiting periods, and that tool is to sacrifice certain things we consider valuable yet weight us down and slow our speed to reaching the finishing line. Your ability to deal with these challenges in the waiting period opens the way for the fulfilment of your dreams. Let us now consider some things worth sacrificing in the waiting period in order to birth your greatness.

Sacrifice Loads That Can Sink You in the Waiting Period

Assuming you are the captain of a ship; this ship happens to be your life. You will not have smooth sailing at all times. I have walked with God and studied the scriptures for some years now. I have understood that God has the tendency to reveal your destination and your glory to you, but mostly at times, he does not tell you what you have to go through to get there. The reason may be that the process of getting to your destination may scare you and cause you to give up, so he keeps that part from you most of the time. When your ship begins to encounter boisterous storm on the verge of perishing, you have to lighten the load of your ship for easy sailing. It is prudent to throw overboard loads that can sink your ship than to contain them and perish at the end. Life is more precious than the load you have in your ship. The waiting period is a burden by itself, and you cannot afford to add unprofitable load which will sink you at the end. You should be ready to sacrifice the following to avoid the challenge of sinking during your waiting period; oversympathizers, comfort zone, and instant gratification.

a) Oversympathizers

One of the things that you have to sacrifice during your period of waiting is the activities of those who oversympathize with us. Such oversympathy rather weights you down during your waiting period and for that matter causing you to miss the anticipated promise. "You are the average of the five people you spend the most time with," says Jim Rohn.

Some friends can be very good, but you will have to let them go if you want to graduate from the waiting period into the actualization of your destiny. You need friends, but do not let your friends choose you; you have to choose your friends. And above all, choose your destiny and its fulfillment over your friends. Be careful with friends who are oversympathizers. Such friends are poisonous. You may not understand this until you find yourself in a real trouble. Friends that look at your unfortunate situation and make you feel sorry about yourself must be abdicated. They may be good friends all right, but the more you allow such friends to make you feel pity about your circumstances, they end up adulterating you. You may not have an evil thought, but from such friends, you will easily conceive forbidding notions. They may not suggest negative directly to you, but you may be able to deduce unpleasant ideas from what they will say. Sulky thinking will never deliver God's promise to you.

Relinquish friends that do not encourage you in the Lord in your moment of waiting irrespective of the mutual benefits of the friendship.

The story of Job's friends in the Bible is a good illustration for this assertion. Job went into a serious moment of his life when all that he labored for had been taken from him. The Bible says, the time he lost all his possessions and his children, he rend his garment, shaved his hair, fell down upon the ground, and worshipped God, saying he came naked from the womb, naked shall he go. The Lord gave them to him so if He has taken, may his name be glorified. *The Bible says, Job did not talk against God in his situation.* He was again struck with sore of boils from the sole of his feet to the crown of his head. Even his wife asked him to curse God and die, yet the Bible says Job did not sin against God with his mouth. His faith was built on no one else but God.

One day, Job's friends decided to visit him upon hearing the great calamity that had befallen him. As the friends were approaching, they looked at Job from afar, but they could not believe their eyes. They wondered if the person they were seeing was the billionaire they used to know. They rend their garments, sprinkled dust upon themselves, and wept sore. They sat with Job pitying him in silence for seven days. They could not offer any word of encouragement to uplift his broken spirit in the Lord, but they lamented so bitterly, and Job felt so miserable in his spirit. They made Job believe that his misfortune was not normal. They even asked Job to confess if he has committed any sin. Job really felt finished.

The man that the Bible said, he did not talk against God but worshipped Him in his moment of perplexity, began to curse himself and cursed the womb that gave birth to him. He cursed to the extent that he cursed the hour, the day, the month, and the year he was born. He wished the day he was born never existed. He even desired to have died in his mother's womb before birth. He suddenly lost faith in God. At that moment of cursing, he felt there was no lifting up for him. How could this be? Because his friends oversympathized with him. One of them probably asked him, "So are you not the one that used to feed the poor? Were you not the eye for the blind? How come you are now reduced to nothing?" Words like these from the friends made Job talk against God. Had it not been for the grace of God, Job would have incurred the wrath of God and thereby lose his blessings. The oversympathy of his friends in his trying moment did not help him but rather weighed him down.

We do not go through challenges just because we have sinned or we are under a curse. The Bible says even the righteous fall seven times; so it does not matter how good, holy, or righteous you are. Tough times will come your way. Be strong and go through it. Those times come to reveal you to yourself. Some will shape you. Others will break you to remold you. Many come to strengthen you. Most come to teach you and leave your life with scars of rich experiences. In the end, they will make you proud of yourself. You will later know that it was never your effort but by the grace of God.

There are sometimes we go through certain things that we need love and words of comfort from friends and love ones. It is good, but I want you to know that do not let that get into you so much. Life is war. Live your life as a soldier ready to fight and conquer. You may obtain casualties on your bodies;

that is fine. That makes you a tough soldier. We do not go to war to sleep. We fight until we win, even if we are hit by bullets we keep fighting.

You are in the front file of your life battlefield. This is not the time to play weak. Be strong and shake the challenges off and move on. It is only you and God that really understand what you are going through, so fight your way out. Do not allow friends to sink you by way of petting you instead of giving you the morale from the word of God to move on.

No one can truly understand your pain because no person can put himself or herself in your shoes. You are the only one that wears it. It is interesting when I hear people saying I have been in your situation before or I have walked this path before, and I know how it feels. Then they begin to sympathize with you. Until a person is thinking like you are thinking and on the same frequency with you in mindset, limited by what is limiting you, having the same options as you, seeing things exactly as you see them, knows only what you know and can do exactly what you can do only in your hard times, trust me, that person does not have a clue of what you are dealing with or going through. There are sometimes words cannot express the pain we find ourselves in. It is only the soul and the spirit that can express what we truly feel inwardly. For these reasons, we should not allow others to make us lose ourselves in our periods of waiting.

Most friends would love to pity you not because they care but because they want you to be pitied among men all the time so they can rise above you. The Bible says David was a man who used to encourage himself in the Lord. He never resorted to men's sympathy. Learn to encourage yourself in the Lord. You can do this by being an addicted student of the Bible.

If you do not sacrifice those that over console you, they will lure you to sacrifice your destiny. By their words and actions, you will desire to help yourself. You may curse yourself and give up waiting on God before the delivery of your miracle. I pray that will not be your portion in Jesus Christ name. Cleave to those that will encourage you in the Lord in times of problem than those who out of pity will cause you to sink.

b) Comfortzone

Another challenge that we have to overcome in our waiting moments is our comfort zone, and we overcome it by sacrificing this comfort zone.

From the introduction, I mentioned that the waiting period comes with restlessness. You should be like a soldier. No soldier at a warfront lives in a comfort zone. No soldier thinks outside the war. He stays focused, very much alert, aggressive, and ready to combat. Being in the comfort zone makes you lazy and relaxed. Comfort zone makes you love yourself more than loving your destiny. You can easily give up in your comfort zone because you may not be ready to go through pain. At the slightest pain, you will give up and say it is ridiculous to go through hard times for your greatness. Any good and trained soldier can set traps and lay ambush for the opponent for hours, days, even months. He will patiently wait until he has seen victory over his enemy before he thinks about his comfort. Let a soldier fall prey to soldier ants, he would not mind. Why? Because he will not rest until he defeats his enemy. How do you expect to win the battle of waiting period if you do not come out of your comfort zone? Consider the waiting period as a war zone. The only way to come out of it victoriously is to sacrifice your comfort zone.

One of the things that makes the eagle so powerful is that it prepares its eyrie on the tallest tree above the canopy of the jungle or in mountains. The location of its eyrie can expose it to certain weather conditions that are not as comfortable as the other birds beneath the canopy of the jungle. Yet the eagle chooses to live there. This animal lives outside its comfort zone for good visibility and easy soaring. It is hard on itself and that makes it tough and ready for every adversity that comes it way.

Accepting to live in your comfort zone during your waiting period is accepting to become an ordinary person, to die an ordinary death, to be buried in an ordinary grave, and to be forgotten as an ordinary person.

Reduce the number of hours you sleep. Invest in knowledge. Do not just buy books; read them and apply the principles in them. Study new things. Add value to your life every day. Be hard on yourself now that you can else life will be hard on you when you have no strength. It is very ugly for life to be hard on you. If I were you, I would choose to train myself the hard way and progress so I can have comfort tomorrow. If you do not work today to rest tomorrow, you will rest today to work very hard tomorrow. "It is always better to have it and not need it than to need it and not have it at all," says Rodger Carter

Invest in your spiritual life as well. Life is spiritual. As you grow in knowledge, be sure to grow in spirit, else the spiritual life will cheat you in the physical. Spend time to study the Bible and pray. These spiritual exercises are the powerhouse for greatness.

We do not sleep during our waiting period. We search for opportunities. We get ourselves ready for what we anticipate to have. We do not just stay idle, eat, watch TV, and waste our time in the name of waiting. That is a deadly adventure.

c) Instant gratification

Another challenge that we have to overcome in our waiting period is instant gratification, and we overcome it by sacrificing what instantly gratifies us.

Will you trade gold for ordinary marbles? Instant gratification is like pleasing your enemies at your expense.

My dear, take your time and build your life. Do not rush. Gratification should come effortlessly, and it should be permanent. It is not possible to build a mansion in just a day. It will collapse and kill you at the end. You are not in competition with anyone. "In God's own time He will make everything beautiful."

It is suicidal to use your seed to prepare a meal to dine and drink with the rich and stay hungry for the rest of your life. You have to be willing to stay hungry now. Sow in tears and reap with joy. Eating your seed will never fill your stomach; it will rather weigh you down until it emaciates you.

Instant gratification is one of the chronic diseases that kill people in the waiting period. Desire for flash gratification can make you rush the process. It can put you in a huge debt.

No matter how you live your life, people will talk about you. Just be you and wait for the right time. The most painful thing in life is to force yourself to show off and become poor later. You can become a laughingstock to those you pleased, so what is the point in it. Kill instant gratification and wait because it can kill you at the end.

Using Altar Sacrifice to Lubricate Divine Response in Your Period of Waiting

It is very true that God delivers his promises in his own time. However, there are some instances we should know what we ought to do in our time of waiting for quick delivery of our miracle. It can be naturally difficult as humans to keep waiting if God does not intervene on time. I mentioned in the introduction that it is not easy to wait, that is why many wish to avoid the waiting period. In some cases, we are permitted to invite God to come to our aid when our strength is weary. This is why sometimes we are expected to do altar sacrifice in our waiting period for heaven to respond swiftly, for us not to become overburdened and miss our miracle. Waiting under harsh conditions without the hope of ever getting closer to the finishing line can be disappointing. As we offer acceptable sacrifice for the speedy intervention of God, we get assurance of getting closer to our ultimate goal.

There was a time in the lives of the Israelites when they were slaves to the then perverse Egyptians. The children of Israel were born free, but everywhere in the land of Egypt, they were in chains. They were subjected to pain, hunger, beating, killing of their young male children, all under the tyrannical rule of the then Pharaoh. The people of Israel were waiting for their deliverer. They cried to the God of their fathers to deliver them. Finally, their cry got to God in heaven. He sent Moses to go back to Egypt to deliver his people and take them to the Promise Land.

Before the Israelites could be released by Pharaoh, there was the need for one big blow from God to shake Pharaoh so that he would let the people go. God said according to Exodus 11:1, He is going to release the killer blow to Pharaoh and the whole land of Egypt. But before He did it, the people of Israel sacrificed. All the nine earlier plagues God brought on Pharaoh could not make Pharaoh let the people of Israel go.

Perhaps the people of Israel wondered if there was any other thing God could do to make Pharaoh let them go. The answer was yes! There was another thing God could do, but it had a price tag of sacrifice. God commanded Moses to tell the people of Israel to kill sheep and paint their blood on their doorpost and eat the meat in the night. God commanded every household to kill an animal. Even a house that cannot kill an animal should join resources with another smaller house and kill an animal. A house that refuses to kill an animal will suffer the same plague as the Egyptians.

My dear, the animals that were killed were sacrifices the children of Israel offered onto the Highest. They offered those sacrifices for divinity to come down into the affairs of humanity to settle the matter in their favor. Among all the plagues that God brought on the Egyptians, the people of Israel sacrificed nothing. The moment God demanded sacrifice from the people of Israel, He executed the deadly plague which Pharaoh could not stand. After God had killed the first-born of the Egyptians because of the sacrifice, Pharaoh could not wait until the following morning. Right in the middle of the night, Pharaoh summoned Moses and Aaron and said to them "Up! Leave my people, you and the Israelites!" (Exodus 12:31b, NIV) Glory to God! Why could Pharaoh not wait till the morning? He realized, if he further delays, he may lose his own life and the lives of his people. What provoked God to do that? It was the sacrifice of his people. This kind of sacrifice was for a particular desire. With this kind of sacrifice, God comes on the scene to do but a specific thing for which the sacrifice was offered.

The people of Israel were seriously waiting to be delivered from bondage. They had prayed for so many years. Their cry had finally gotten to God in heaven but still they were in bondage. I know you might be in bondage right now. You may be waiting for your deliverance. You may be crying and asking God from whence cometh your help. Have you tried the power in sacrifice as you await your moment of deliverance? God has seen your cry. He has heard your prayer as He heard that of the Israelites. What are you willing to do to provoke divinity to come into your affairs? Sacrifices on the altar of God speaks volumes. The moment you put down an acceptable sacrifice on the altar of God, you are there and then entitled to receive response from God. It is automatic. Sacrifice is used to touch God in a mysterious way that makes Him show himself strong. The moment you offer an acceptable sacrifice to God, He becomes restless and uncomfortable in his seat. He only rests after releasing blessings or attending to the need of the one that gave it.

The purpose of the sacrifice that God demanded from the Israelites was to quicken their delivery in the waiting period. God knows that as humans it is sometimes hard for us to wait beyond what we can endure, that is why He gives us such opportunity to invite Him through sacrifice for swift response.

The ultimate sacrifice you can give to God in your waiting period is yourself. Present yourself a living sacrifice, holy and acceptable unto God. God needs your heart more than your money.

*Great achievement is usually born of great
sacrifice and is never the result of selfishness.*

Chapter 3

Prayer

*If you only pray when you are in
trouble, then you are in trouble.*

Apart from *patience* and *sacrifice* as some of the tools used in dealing with the challenges we encounter in our waiting period, the next tool we are going to consider is *prayer*.

According to the scriptures, if there is any that is merry, let him sing. Is there any that is sick, let him call upon the elders of the church to pray for him and anoint him, and he shall be healed. But is there any that is in *pain*, let that person *pray*! Prayer is the antidote for pain, life turmoil, and other forms of hurricanes that hit us in this journey of life. It is by prayer that we bulldoze our way through impenetrable walls and plough our paths through satanic traps. Until you become addicted to prayer and pray continuously, you will not achieve massive success. The one that prays a lot is always active in the spiritual realms and gets stronger as the day goes by. The forces in the dark kingdom will not allow you to be great unto the glory of God unless you pray your way to the top. Anybody in a waiting period is going through a great deal of pain that people cannot see but only God and himself. No one will be able to understand the pain of a waiting man except God. I want to tell you that one of the tools that is a must to deploy when dealing with the challenges of waiting is *prayer*. The Bible makes us understand that we should go to the Lord in prayer and cast all our burdens on him.

According to Pastor John Haggue, a Christian sees far on his knees in prayer than standing without praying. Prayer keeps you in charge of the situation. True prayer will give you a sense of relief, and you will not be carried away by the circumstances in your waiting period. If you really want to successfully go through your waiting period and be celebrated, then go down on your knees in prayer.

The truth is, you do wrestle but not with flesh and blood. You wrestle with powers of the underworld, rulers of darkness, principalities, and demonic kingdoms. These are powerful entities who are so determined to make sure you fail woefully in your life. They are very powerful and, above all, wicked beyond measure. Do you know what it means to fight with principalities? They are princes and princesses of demonic and territorial spheres. They are royals in the demonic kingdom. They carry weight and have much power. They make decisions and make laws in the affairs of humanities. Witches and wizards go no close to them in terms of rank. Satan himself is the prince of darkness. If you do not become addicted to prayer, they will destroy every good thing in your life. Sometimes, you need to pray an agonizing prayer, offensive prayer, defensive prayer, supplication prayer, etc.

Satan and his cohorts are supernaturally powerful. One of these principalities was powerful enough to arrest and imprison a holy angel sent by God to deliver the prayer answers of Daniel for three weeks. The *prince* from the context of the scriptures is translated as *captain*. We are dealing with ancient captains who are embodiments of wickedness.

They are also powerful in high places. Do not deceive yourself that if you just do good and live a normal life you are good to go. They do not care about living a good life. The food they eat is to see you cry, suffer, live your life in bondage, and destroy you. The only person they are afraid of is a fervent praying child of God filled with power and fire. Satan will not clap for you if you want to fulfill your destiny, impact lives positively, and help humanity. He will fight you with all the power that he has. He will throw arrows and spears at you. He will strategically design weapons for your destruction. The enemies we are dealing with are extremely dangerous than terrorists. They feed off your pain and rejoice over your loss. They are happy to see you down in life. Just wake up and pray like never before. The good news is, the God that Christians pray to is more than powerful and more than capable to bring down satanic kingdom. He is Almighty. He is always attentive to the prayer of his children. His ears are widely open to your prayers. Whatever that is killing you, take it to Him in prayer as you wait.

With God, nothing is impossible. What are you waiting for that He cannot give to you? He tells us to ask in faith without wavering, and we will be given. Do you need healing or supernatural provision? God is ever ready to release them if you will just ask in prayer. No good thing will He withhold from those that diligently seek him in prayer.

Prayer will not just aid you to successfully go through your waiting period. It has the power to bring your miracle from the supernatural into the natural. The most powerful man is the one who can pray to God for his prayer to be answered.

I tried it and it worked. I got to a situation in my life where it was only prayer that saved me. By prayer, the Lord brought me to America. I was praying more than twenty-four hours a week continually. My father, Rev. Richard Oduro, would not let me relax but to pray. I prayed like never before. The consular that interviewed me for my USA visa asked me a question and answered it for me without hearing what I had to say. Then she said my visa was approved.

Before my visa interview, I prayed myself into America. When I got to the embassy, every staff I met, including the consular that interviewed me, was smiling at me in a friendly manner as if they knew me. The way they were greeting me and asking me how I was doing was just awesome. When I was supposed to greet them, they would greet me instead.

I entered the embassy with a kind of fire and a new version of me. I was a changed man when I entered. A man can change himself in prayer (Luke 9:29). If only you will pray continually, you will see the hand of God in that marriage. Wake up and pray in the night and bring your children before God, and they will be delivered from all kinds of demonic powers. We are in times when demons are making children rebellious and breaking homes. Do not just wait and hope it will be alright; burn the midnight oil in prayer to save your home and your destiny.

This story about Elijah and Ahab in the bible better amplifies the place of prayer in dealing with the challenges of our waiting period.

> And it came to pass after many days, that the word of the LORD came to Elijah in the third year, saying, Go, shew thyself unto Ahab; I will send rain upon the earth.
>
> And Elijah said unto Ahab, Get thee up, eat and drink; for there is a sound of abundance of rain. So Ahab went up to eat and to drink. And Elijah went up to the top of Carmel; and he cast himself down upon the earth, and put his face between his knees, And said to his servant, Go up now, look toward the sea. And he went up, and looked, and said,

There is nothing. And he said, Go again seven times. And it came to pass at the seventh time, that he said, Behold, there ariseth a little cloud out of the sea like a man's hand. And he said, Go up, say unto Ahab, prepare thy chariot, and get thee down, that the rain stop thee not. And it came to pass in the meanwhile, that the heaven was black with clouds and wind, and there was a great rain. And Ahab rode and went to Jezreel. (1 Kings 18:1, 41–45)

God gave Prophet Elijah a promise to send down rain to the land. The prophet also told the king that he hears the sound of an abundant rain. The land has been dried for years. No sign of rain, yet he said he hears the sound of abundant rain. Maybe your life is so dry, but the word of God said Jesus became poor so that you can become rich. You have to believe and see with your spiritual eyes that you are not poor. The prophet believed in the word of God. He was actually waiting for the rain that God promised. In fact, the king and the entire nation were all waiting for the rain.

The Bible says Elijah cast himself upon the earth on Mount Carmel. He knew that just waiting for the rain was not enough, so he travailed in prayer to give birth to the rain God talked about.

Elijah prayed for hours but there was no rain. One may ask, was it not God that promised to send down rain? So why the delay? It was God, but there are some promises that can only be delivered on the wings of persistent prayer. Perhaps if Elijah had not prayed the way he did, he would have waited forever. Between the time God promised to send down the rain and the time the rain came was a waiting period. If Elijah had resorted to eating, drinking, and sleeping, he might have not seen the glory of God. By persistent prayer, he ended the waiting period in victory. The land that was very dry became wet.

God has given you so many promises in his word. Do not say because he has said it, he will do it so you will wait without praying. Remember, the same way you are waiting for your blessings, the same way your enemy is working against you.

Do not just wait in waiting but pray persistently in waiting.

Through Prayer You Will Get the Strength From God to Finish in Victory

The taste of finishing is always sweet. The act of finishing hard means one can easily give up at the verge of finishing, so he should put in the best effort to become victorious. Without strength, you will faint and give up. By prayer, you will obtain enough strength to conquer the war of a waiting period. The ultimate goal of Jesus Christ coming into the world was to go to the cross. It was not just about the miracles He performed. It got to a time that it was hard for him to go to the cross. He wished not to die for us at a point. He beheld the pain and the torture He would go through. The Son of God needed strength to endure and to finish. By the prayer in the garden of Gethsemane, Jesus received strength from above and He finished victoriously. All the years Jesus walked on earth doing signs and wonders were in his waiting period. He was actually preparing to go to the cross. If the Lamb of God had not given himself to prayer in those years to receive strength from God, things might have gone wrong.

Moving from your waiting period into your destiny will never be easy for you without prayer. Rev. Richard Oduro told me this in Ghana before leaving for the USA, "If you had not prayed the way you did after the prophecy, you would not have received your visa" (ref. 1 Timothy 1:18). It seems so hard to pray because prayer is a weapon not meant for children's use. Prayer does mind-blowing things, so try it in your moment of waiting.

By prayer, Joshua asked God to make time stand still until he defeats his enemies, and it was granted. Have you considered what it means for the sun to stand still? The whole cosmic and the entire universe is in constant motion. The planets revolve around the sun in our solar system. The entire solar system is in motion within the Milky Way. When Joshua prayed for the sun to stand still, it was not just the sun that stood still. It was the entire cosmic body because they are all intertwined. By prayer, a man could stop the hand of time and halt the motion of the heavens. Is there anything that prayer cannot do? The fact that you are not getting results does not mean it does not work. Maybe you have to consider the way you pray. By prayer, Elijah called *fire* from heaven to consume not only a bull sacrifice, but also the stones used to make the altar of the sacrifice and licked up about twelve barrels of water in the trench. Is that not wonderful? King Hezekiah was in a hopeless situation. At that moment, he was waiting for the deliverance of his people from Sennacherib, King of Assyria. Assyrian soldiers wanted to slaughter the children of Judah. Hezekiah pulled out his greatest weapon—prayer. By that prayer, God released an angel to kill one hundred and eighty-five thousand Assyrian soldiers in just one night. If one man could pray to kill almost a whole army of a country, then you can too. By prayer Hannah gave birth to prominent children after waiting to become a mother for years.

Faith in the Faithfulness of God

Prayer is a great artillery when dealing with the challenges of waiting, but it calls *for faith in the faithfulness of God* for it to work for you. The Bible says, he that prays but not in faith is like the waves of the seas. Such person will receive nothing from God.

> God is not a man that he should lie; neither the son of man that he should repent: hath he said and shall he not do it? Or hath he spoken, and shall he not make it good? (Numbers 23:19 KJV)

Having absolute trust and confidence in the abilities of God is paramount in your waiting period. I wonder how you can have a plenary conviction in the provision of God if you do not have faith in his faithfulness. As you pray, believe in the fidelity of God.

Know that God cannot lie. Understanding that all his promises are yea and amen gives you hope beyond hope that God will answer your prayer in the period of waiting. The faithfulness of God is sure. If God could create all the things, you can possibly think of, both physical and spiritual, what then can He not do? If you believe He can do all things, and He said ask and it shall be given, do you think He will lie about that? Some of the things you can dare God, and no matter what He cannot do is to lie. Just have faith in the faithfulness of God that He cannot lie. And whatever you are praying and waiting for will be delivered to you in Jesus' name.

If you have tried all things and it did not work, I dare you to try prayer in the waiting period for it works. It will give you the strength to keep moving forward. It will cause rain to fall on the dry land of your life. It is naturally impossible for one to conceive and give birth on the same day; but keep praying for if God willeth, you will birth your greatness today because as Zion travailed in prayer, she brought forth her children in a day. So can you, for our God is the same yesterday, today, and forevermore. Just have faith in His faithfulness.

Sometimes, all it takes is one prayer
to change everything.

Chapter 4

Extra Oil from the Holy Spirit

To fight, we must have oil for our machine.

This chapter is introducing us to another tool in dealing with the challenges of waiting and that is extra oil from the Holy Spirit.

It is the extra oil that can help you to walk in darkness until you get to the end of the tunnel. Most of us do not have extra oil. We are only depending on the little oil in our tanks. That is why most of us give up when we are faced with diverse temptations in our waiting period. Remember I told you in the introduction that the matured are able to wait irrespective of the length of the waiting period. It is only possible to wait when you have extra oil from the Holy Spirit.

The waiting period can be likened to a man who is lost in a vast desert and trying to find his way home. If the man does not have enough water to sustain him, he will probably die without ever making it home. The journey of waiting can be far depending on several factors for an individual.

Then shall the kingdom of heaven be likened unto ten virgins, which took their lamps, and went forth to meet the bridegroom. And five of them were wise and five of them were foolish. They that were foolish took their lamps and took no (extra) oil with them. But the wise took (extra) oil in their vessels with their lamps. While the bridegroom tarried, they all slumbered and slept. And at the midnight there was a cry made, behold the bridegroom cometh; go ye out to meet him. Then all the virgins arose and trimmed their lamps. And the foolish said unto the wise, give us of your oil; for our lamps are gone out. But the wise answered, saying, not so; lest there be not enough for us and you: but go ye rather to them that sell, and buy for yourselves. And while they went to buy, the bridegroom came; and they that were ready went in with him to the marriage: and the door was shut. Afterward came also the other virgins, saying, Lord, Lord open to us. But he answered and said, verily I say unto you, I know you not. (Matthew 25:1–12)

Although the above scripture is a parable talking about the second coming of Christ Jesus, but I wish to appropriate it to my message in another context. What is your bridegroom in life? What good thing are you waiting for? Sometimes, we do not prepare adequately for what we hope to have one day. Due to poor preparation in life, most of us grope for our desires.

The ten virgins prepared by putting oil in their lamps, but those that were with extra oil were those that extra prepared. Preparation is a whole chapter in this book, so I will not talk much about it here. I want you to bear in mind that whatever you are aiming at needs extra preparation. All the ten virgins prepared, but five of them did not prepare adequately. How prepared are you for what you are waiting for? Extra preparation can serve as an alternative plan. Your first plan might fail but you should not be found wanting. You should be able to position yourself in alignment with your destination and press toward it. The wise anticipated that the journey might be long, so they took extra oil.

The oil used to fuel lamps in the olden days was olive oil. Olive oil is used to symbolize the Holy Spirit. You need the Holy Spirit to fill you up so you can obtain strength to fight the battle of waiting. Without the strength of the Holy Spirit, your lamp will go off, and you will walk in darkness and end up falling into a pit.

The oil gives your lamp the power to light. Without the oil, the lamp will not light. The light gives vision, and therefore, light is vision. This means, the oil is the source of vision. You cannot wait if you do not have a vision of what you are waiting for. Clear vision is a kind of power that will inspire you to do all things possible to victoriously come out of your waiting period. No matter how long your waiting period may seem, you will wait because of the vision you have.

Many people are actually waiting for what they do not see. The very thing some people are waiting for passes them by every day because they have no vision of what they need. Those that *pass over opportunities regularly* are always *POOR* because they have no vision. If the Holy Spirit is not the source and the sustainer of your vision, then you have failed already.

The wise had extra zeal and determination in their heart. They did not want to return until they accomplished the mission of the journey. Life is a journey. As you wait for your desire, you need to have a bold heart like a lion and a tough skin like a crocodile. Due to their determination, they did not want to encourage distractions. They knew that shortage of oil could prevent them from meeting the bridegroom; hence, they armed themselves with extra oil. The foolish virgins just set off. Do not entertain evil thoughts and bad counsel from friends as you wait for your greatness. Be positive, be zealous, and be determined to do it. God will also help you.

The wise knew that their lives depended on the accomplishment of the mission. Should they fail in the mission, their lives have come to an end. They would rather abort anything that may try to abort their mission. That was why they refused to share their extra oil with the foolish virgins. If the foolish virgins were really serious in meeting the bridegroom, they could have walked in the footsteps of the wise to meet the groom. Whatever you are waiting for, do not just wait but do anything honorable to achieve it because your life and others depend on it. Your success is a blessing for many, so do not fail. They did not know their lives depended on meeting the groom until they lost him. There are some people you will have to let go if you want to accomplish your mission. The wise virgins had to let go of the foolish virgins to enable them to finish their task. Until you have the taste of finishing, you will never respect yourself. Accomplish your waiting period successfully. Failure in your waiting period is equivalent to failure in life.

It is okay to be wearied in your period of waiting as a human being, but do not lose the battle. Even the wise virgins got tired of waiting in the night and fell asleep, but the most important thing is they did not miss the groom.

The foolish virgins were on a journey to meet their bridegroom. At one point, they had to wait for the bridegroom. For poor preparation and lack of determination to accomplish the mission, they journeyed in vain. By the time they returned from buying the extra oil, it was too late for them to be allowed into the banquet hall. I pray you do not wait in vain. This is the time that you can make a conscious effort and take good decisions to affect your life positively. Do not let things go bad and say had I known. The Holy Bible tells us to do things in the times that we can before the bad years catch up with us. As you are in your waiting period, take time to prepare yourself adequately for opportunities. Be determined to win. The wise virgins did not know the exact time for the groom's arrival, but they were able to meet the groom. No matter how long it takes. Make sure you meet your groom in life. Do not give up. If you want to positively affect lives, then I dare you not to give up. Have the virtues of the wise virgins, and you will not miss the target in Jesus Christ name.

Keep fighting even in the mist of your problem as you wait. Victory is close to those that strategically keep fighting to the end. Keep your head up. Although you are hard pressed, you are not crashed. You may be in your deepest perplexity but not in despair. Persecuted but not forgotten. You may be struck down but never knocked out. Fight the good fight of waiting, and you will get the crown of glory. This crown of glory always goes to those that are able to endure to the end. If one can endure, he or she needs extra oil from the Holy Spirit.

The one that has oil has more than oil.

Chapter 5

Faith Declaration

Speak faith and then watch your faith work for you.

Life and death are in the hands of the tongue. If you are able to successfully deal with the challenges in the waiting period, then you should be mindful of what you say during your waiting period. Faith declaration is another important tool to tackle the challenges of waiting. Whatever you declare must be based on the word of God because that is the only word that carries absolute authority.

People are saying you are forsaken. Many are those that think you will never rise up. Your own family members despise you because you do not have money. Your friends say you are a failure. You have heard all the things that people have to say about you, and my question is, what is being said about you by the Highest Authority in the entire universe?

Do not accept any identity people will tag you with just because you are in your waiting period. Know what your Lord and Master Christ Jesus says about you and tag yourself with that.

The other day, God took prophet Ezekiel into a valley of bones in a vision. The Lord asked him to go round the bones and assess the condition of them. When Ezekiel did his assessment, he saw that the bones were very dry beyond hope according to the eyes of man. God asked Ezekiel whether the bones could live. Ezekiel saw that humanly it is not possible, but he knew that with God all things are possible, hence he responded that "God thou knowest."

I hereby tell you that God is the final decision taker in your life. It can be for a fact that your life is as dry as a bone. It may be for a fact that you are not important in society, but the truth is, you are more than important in Christ Jesus. There is a difference between fact and truth. It can be a fact that you are weak, but the truth is you are strong in Christ. Let people talk about the fact while you declare the truth about you from the scriptures. It can be for a fact that you are poor. There is no hope of ever making money, but the Bible says let the poor say I am rich. That is the truth. The word of God tells you who you truly are. Let God be true, and every man becomes a liar. These words are not to flatter you. They are spirit and truth. If you believe it, confess it out of conviction, and take action toward it, you will be wealthy beyond your imagination.

Even if you are at the bottom of life. God has the power through Jesus Christ to bring you back to your destined position. The dry bones represented the lives of the people of Israel. They were cast on the ground and were being trampled upon. They thought that was their end. There was no hope for them, but when the King of Kings, the CEO of all things, the Commander in Chief of all creations, came to the scene. He spoke and dry bones came back to life. I love what Prophet Ezekiel said in chapter 37 verse 4b, "Dry bones, hear the word of the Lord!" (NIV). The words spoken in the prophecy to command life into the dry bones were not words from Ezekiel but words of the Most High. Wow!

Do you see dryness in any aspects of your life? Are you cast down? Speak the word of God into your life in the name of Yeshua Hamashiach. Stand in the shoes of Prophet Ezekiel this minute and tell whatever problem it is to listen but to the word of God not your words. Speak the words of God in your waiting period that says the one who was, who is, and is to come. That says the one that all powers bow down to. Let every dead thing in your life come back to life in the name of Jesus Christ. Let there be tendons, flesh, skin, and breath of life from God fill every dry bone in your life in the name of Jesus. My dear, just open your mouth and speak the word. Proclaim and claim the power in God's word. That says the Lord. Hallelujah.

Do not shut your mouth about the word in your moment of waiting. Let me tell you something. God has spoken. He has released the blessings and the protections. Sometimes we become ignorant of who we are, and the devil capitalizes on it to torment our lives. *Learn how to speak words of faith in the season of waiting.* Other people cannot understand what you are going through but God understands.

In your waiting, tell yourself it will be all right. Encourage yourself in the Lord as King David used to do. God did not bring you through all the predicaments you faced in the past to disgrace you at this moment of your life. You are more than a conqueror through him that loves you. You can do all things through Christ who strengthens you. The Lord is your light and your salvation. Why should you fear? The Lord is the strength of your life of whom should you be afraid. Even if the devil and his cohorts come against you to eat up your flesh, they will stumble and fall. Should the whole world reject you and come against you, do not fear; be confident for the Lord is with you.

It is written that Christ Jesus came to take your place in poverty for you to be rich, so claim it. It is written that there is now no condemnation to them that are in Christ Jesus, so any condemnation from your family background against you is nullified. It is also written that God will supply all your needs according to his riches in glory in Christ Jesus, so just put your plans into action, and by faith God will supply your needs. It is again written that the Lord is your shepherd so how can you want. It is still written that there shall be none barren in the house of God so expect your babes. The scriptures cannot lie, so confess them and appropriate the blessings in them for your life.

Let us learn something so profound in the scriptures.

> Why do the nations conspire and the people plot in vain? The Kings of the earth take their stand and the rul-ers gather together against the Lord and against his anointed one. Let us

break his chains they say and throw off his fetters. The one enthroned in heaven laughs; the Lord scoffs at them. He rebukes them in His anger and terrifies them in His wrath saying, I have installed my King on Zion, my holy hill. I will proclaim the decree of the Lord; He said to me, you are my son today I have become your father. Ask of me and I will make the nations your inheritance and the ends of the earth your possession. (Psalms 2:1–8)

From the above scripture, enemies were conspiring against David. They wanted to destroy his life and scatter all his plans. The reason why the enemies attempted to destroy David in the first place was that they did not know who David was. They had no idea that the Ancient of days had adopted David as a son. It was in the verse 7 that David said he will declare the decree of the Lord. The Lord made a decree to David that He has adopted him as a son but not only that, he should ask of Him the nations and He will give them as inheritance and the ends of the earth as his possession.

Until David declared the decree of God about himself, his enemies were busy plotting against him. Do not keep your mouth shut. The moment you start to declare the decrees of God in the scriptures about you, the devil and his cohorts run from you. The word of God that comes out of the mouth of God's children are more powerful than intercontinental ballistic missiles. Nuclear weapons cannot be compared to the "dunamis" of God's word. God's word comes out of our mouth like a double-edged sword. The devils are afraid of it, so use it.

When you find yourself in problems, do not keep quiet about who you are. You are the child of the Most High, and He says ask of Him and He will give you the nations as inheritance. Confess the decrees of the Lord about your life and the devil will run from you. Do not keep quiet. Let the world know who you are in Christ Jesus as you wait. Do not play timidly. You are a child of a lion. Let the lion in you roar and the fake lions like the demons will disappear.

It is so sweet to trust in Jesus, to hold him just by his word. Rest upon his promises to you. Hold onto the word. Do not let the words leave your mouth and heart. Ponder over it day and night, and your ways shall be prosperous. As you confess faith in your life, your declarations will see you through the waiting period.

If you are sinking in your waiting period. I recommend you declare words of faith in the Lord. This will trigger the release of God's strength into your life and again give you hope in the Lord. As Job did, he confessed his faith in the Lord, "I know my redeemer lives…if there is hope even for a tree that is cut down and the roots dried up in the ground and the stock thereof dies, it will surely bud through the scent of water and bring forth again." Job's faith declaration was the anchor of his life in his period of crisis. Speak faith and declare positive things for yourself in your waiting period because you are what you say.

The stars may fall but God's promises will stand and be fulfilled.

Chapter 6

Give Thanks and Rejoice in Waiting

God gave you a gift of 86,400 seconds today. Have you used one to say, "Thank you, God?"

Although the fig tree shall not blossom, neither shall fruit be in the vines; the labour of the olive shall fail, and the fields shall yield no meat; the flock shall be cut off from the fold, and there shall be no herd in the stall: Yet I will rejoice in the Lord, I will joy in the God of my salvation. The Lord God is my strength, and he will make my feet like hinds' feet, and he will make me to walk upon mine high places. To the chief

singer on my stringed instruments.
(Habakkuk 3:17–19 KJV)

Give thanks when all odds are against you. Let your thanksgiving come out of a grateful heart. The Bible says that in all things give thanks to the creator and the owner of all things. As we read in the book of Habakkuk, maybe you have lost your main stream of income. You may be facing rejection from loved ones. Possibly you are suffering from abuse in your marriage or other relationships that you want it fixed. Are your children going wayward that you need them to become responsible? The Bible says, rejoice in the Lord. This situation you find yourself in is your waiting period. There is hope for the living. Positive things are attracted to people with cheerful vibes. Thank God in all situations.

Thanksgiving should be a way of life. It should not be on a condition for what you are desiring. God desires your thanks given, praises, and worship. As you do that, you call his divine presence to be with you all the time. It is expected of us to rejoice in Him, thank and worship Him all the time. In so doing, He gives us our heart's desires and gives unto us things that we have not even thought of or asked from Him. It is written, things that we have no idea of, thought of, and imagined is what the father has prepared for them that love him.

Praises and Worship Release Unexpected Miracles

When it comes to worship, praise, and rejoicing in him, it should not just be for the fact that you are in your waiting period. Whether you are rich or poor, sick or healthy, just thank and worship God. It should be a voluntary outward and inward expression of love to Him. Know that it is your duty to thank God always. As you understand this and do that, His presence continues to be with you, and He gives you things you have not even thought of. When Paul and Silas were in prison, the Bible says they sang songs of praises unto God, and immediately, there was a great earthquake, and the foundation of the prisons shook, and the doors and the bonds were loosened on them all. The truth is, Paul and Silas did not praise God because they wanted God to release them from the prison. They could not help it than to praise God even in bondage. It was in their DNA irrespective of the situation they found themselves. If praising God was with the intention of gaining freedom from the prison, they would have left immediately after the power of God had released them. But instead, they did not take a step and even cautioned the prison warden not to harm himself.

Should there be peace in your life or not. Should there be money in your bank account or not. Whatever it is. Just choose to praise and worship God in faithfulness, and you will be surprised at what the Lord will do in your life. In praising and worshiping him in the moment of waiting, He will give you deliverance as He gave to Paul and Silas.

> The joy of the Lord is your strength. (Nehemiah 8:10d)

Praising and worshiping God in truth and in spirit sends joy into the throne room of God. Anytime undiluted praises and worship hit the throne room of God, He discharges strength to where the praise emanates from because of the joy that He feels. His glory also comes down to saturate the life of the one that sings praises to Him. Having strength from God and being engulfed with His glory is essential for a period such as waiting. By the strength of God, you will never faint in your waiting period, and by His glory, your victory in the waiting period is assured.

Do not allow what you are dealing with to take the praises and the worship of God from your life. I know it is hard. Life is actually hard. The thing that makes success beautiful and sweet is choosing to go the hard way that others would not go, which sets you apart from the lot.

> He is fearful in praise. (2 Chronicles 20:22)

Sometimes, our waiting periods are orchestrated by enemies and wicked spirits. The instance you begin to sing songs of encomiums, God becomes charged. Should there be any form of devilish encroachment in your territory, His holy indignation boils up and fight on your behalf. This alone can bring an end to the challenge in your waiting period. Just by praises and worship, King Jehoshaphat went to battle and won without lifting a sword to fight. God is very fearful in praises. Learn to praise Him in the waiting period.

Being happy in the Lord even as you wait gives you supernatural promotion as in the case of David.

Let me share with you one of the secrets of King David. In the book of Psalm 23 verse 1 through 6. David said the Lord is his shepherd; he shall not want.

He makes him lie down in green pasture. He leads him to the still waters. He restores his soul. God leads him in the paths of righteousness for His name's sake. This guy was walking through the valley of the shadow of death, yet he said, he will fear no evil; for God is with him. God's rod and staff comforts him. Then he said. God prepares a table for him in the presence of his enemies. The Lord anoints his head with oil. His cup runs over. Then he ends by saying goodness and mercy shall follow him all the days of his life, and he shall dwell in the house of the Lord forever. Wow!

Let me attempt to give you a certain picture of David in Psalm 23. This was a guy who was a bush boy. Rejected by his parents and siblings. Left alone to take care of sheep in the wilderness all by him-self. When it rained, he had to find a tree and hide beneath it. He had no shelter and the sun scorched at him all the time. If David heard any sound, it would be the bleating of sheep, the singing of birds, and the roaring of lions. Bible scholars believe Jesse was not a poor man. He could have hired or bought a slave to take care of his sheep, but he did not. He chose to make his son a slave. The truth is the family did not care whether a wild animal devoured this guy or not.

Upon all these problems, David did not allow his problems to consume him. He was always in praises and worship mood for God. He said the Lord is his shepherd whiles he was a bush boy. At times the bears and lions came and attack him and his sheep, he used to say even though he walks through the valley of the shadow of death, God is with him. In his deepest despair, he takes comfort from the Lord. He said the Lord prepares a table for him in the presence of his enemies, yet he was dining with sheep. Despite all this, David was thanking and praising his maker. God was seated on His throne, and He saw David and made him a man after His own heart. David had problems, but he refused to give attention to the problems. He focused on God and sang praises and worshiped Him all the time. God also lifted him form the bush and made him king.

Learn to praise and rejoice in God in every new day that He gives you. Do not put emphasis on your problem as you wait for good things in your life. Just thank Him from your heart. Worship Him. As you do that, you attract His presence, and you begin to forget about your problems. You will feel so light within you and God will take over. The moment you praise and worship Him, He takes your load and gives you peace in your waiting period.

Praising God in your challenging moment gives you the opportunity for supernatural promotion.

As David kept on praising and worshiping God in his waiting period, he was supernaturally promoted from being a shepherd to become the king of Israel.

Rejoice in the Lord because He rejoices over you with singing.

Chapter 7

Self-Control

The first and greatest victory is to conquer self.

Self-control is one of the effective tools we should not overlook in our waiting period. Self-control in this context is the ability to control yourself in temptations that crop up in our waiting period. We are open to a whole lot of temptations in our period of waiting. Waiting is to make you firm and great at the end. Any product of waiting period is like a fine gold that has passed through fire of purification. The glory thereof is unmatched. Those that are able to win the battle of waiting are seen as extraordinary people. Successful products of waiting period are people of standards used to measure others. You become a role model for millions, and you become a beacon of hope to even those who do not know you if you win the battle of waiting. But remember, no good thing comes cheaply. It is therefore prudent to have self-control and certain kinds of attitudes in your waiting period.

Endurance

As the saying goes, your altitude is determined by your attitude. The kind of attitude you put on in your waiting period is very crucial. It is easy to put on a happy face when all is well. What about when you are in pain?

Having the attitude to go through anything no matter how hard it may be is the kind of attitude great people put out there.

The eagle is one of the animals with a good attitude to learn from. This animal hates to fail, so it makes sure it does anything possible to succeed. It does not mind inflicting pain on itself and waits for the appointed time of its life.

When an eagle grows to a certain stage of its life, the talons and the beak become weak. The feathers produce a noise that signals prey to run to safety. If an eagle gets to this stage of its life, it seldom catches prey. At this stage, it uses the beak to plug out the talons and the feathers. It again hits the beak against a rock until it breaks. Because of its attitude to win at all costs, it inflicts pain on itself. It does not pay attention to the blood that oozes out. It stays in solitude for weeks without food until new feathers, talons, and beak are grown. From this time, when it sets off to haunt, it does not fail.

The weeks of seclusion without food is its waiting period. The pain it goes through as a result of removing the talons, beak, and the weak feathers tells you that going through a waiting period is not a joke. But those that are able to walk through with the attitude of winning are able to soar like the eagle. A mind prepared to endure is capable of soaring above the challenges of waiting. Such a person can never miss greatness. This kind of greatness is so conspicuous that people will not be able to ignore it.

Public Pressure

Allowing yourself to be pushed and prodded by the pressure and opinion of the public is very deadly in your waiting period. People may pressure you to take hasty steps, which in the end will be suicidal. Remember, those that sometimes coerce or pressure people to take hasty decisions never share in the consequences so beware.

King Saul was asked by Prophet Samuel to *wait* for him to come and offer the burnt sacrifice before he goes to war. The soldiers started putting undue pressure on King Saul to offer the sacrifice so they could go to war, else they will all perish. The instruction given to Saul was to *wait* for Samuel no matter what. King Saul was moved by the pressure of the soldiers. He could not wait any longer, so he forced himself to offer the burnt offering. Immediately after that Samuel appeared. By this act of heeding the pressure of the people, the dynasty was taken away from his household. Understand that the people that pushed him to act foolishly did not lose anything, but he lost a throne. It is equally important to be careful and deal wisely with public pressure. Just understand that you are not in competition with anyone in life.

Another biblical figure who yielded to public pressure and failed immensely was Moses. He could not control himself when the people were mounting pressure on him for water. Moses was supposed to stretch forth his rod on the rock, but due to the inordinate pressure that was on him, he did contrary to the instruction of God. By this, Moses could not enter the Promise Land. He was supposed to lead the people to the Promise Land, but he died on the way. People can pressure you to do what you are not supposed to do all in the name of hardship. The pressure may come from your spouse, parents, siblings, or even close friends. Just be careful because in the end, the penalty will fall on you alone. I pray you do not die in your wilderness due to public pressure. Do not allow yourself to be consumed by external pressure. It can cost you dearly. In your waiting period, master self-control.

Control yourself or someone else will control you.

Chapter 8

Preparation

Let today be the start in pursuit of something new.

Why are you idle in the name of waiting? Why are you afraid to start all over again even if you failed at first? Victors of life are those willing to strategize to complete good things in life. You may have great dreams and aspirations, but life will not bring them to you on a silver platter. It calls for work to be done. Do not just wait for waiting's sake. Do not be naive that praying and giving to the poor and reading books to obtain knowledge without planning will give you the result you desire in life. It will never happen like that unless you adequately prepare yourself for it. Do you have faith in God? Do you want your dreams to be fulfilled? Then prepare enough before you start work.

Get up and fight for what is yours. Life will not give you what you want. It will give you what you planned to fight for. You have been waiting for far too long. Fight! Fight! And fight! Until you win. Do not take things as normal. The devil is a liar. Are you telling me you will sit down idle and watch the devil rob you of your job, your marriage, your children, and your money without planning to fight back? You had better fight for your territory. Do not let the size of your enemy scare you. Do not let the distance between your starting point and your destination deter you. The bigger and taller your enemies are, the bigger they fall. You might cry but keep moving forward according to your plan. Keep fighting. Use anything at your disposal to fight for what is yours because your life depends on it. The fight is part of the process, and it will help you stay at the top. Make the fight your friend because life is war. It is so dangerous to get something you did not earn. That is why the waiting period is a must for everybody to go through. If you fight for what you desire, you will not let anybody take it from you. People let go of things so easily because they did not prepare to receive them.

Good Preparation Is a Source of Hope and Strength

Hardly will you faint in your waiting period if you have a workable plan out of it. The feeling that your plan will be successful makes you forget your hardship in the waiting period. It gives you a kind of joy and strength to move forward when all people have lost hope. It makes you feel like there are butterflies in your stomach whenever you look into the future with your mind's eyes. Let people try to discourage you; they will not succeed because of the preparation you have done. This is because you are convinced that your plan will take you to your desired destination. People with good plans end up encouraging people in their waiting period as they try to sympathize with them.

Let me caution you here, the fact that you are expected to plan and add works does not mean you can do it by your own powers. Hear me please— God says it is He that gives you the ability to make wealth. You can do all things by dint of hard work, but if the hand of God is not in it, the watchman watches in vain and the laborer labors for nothing.

Coming out of your waiting period does not mean just living a luxurious life. It means a life of positive impact on the lives of humanity. When we talk of blessing, it is not the cars, the money, the houses, the private jets among others. These are nothing but evidence of riches. It is the blessing of the Lord that makes a man rich. Until you are blessed, you cannot manifest these things. Some people go to the devil for devilish blessing to possess these things, and they always cry at the end. Jacob and Esau never fought over the money, animals, and the other riches of their father, but they fought over the blessing. Why? For without the blessing, man toils in vain. Why is it that most youth nowadays catch the shadow and leave the substance. We chase after money which is the shadow of the real riches. Real riches are a product of the blessing of God upon the lives of people. Without that you can do nothing. It is better to be prepared for an opportunity which may never come than to get an opportunity unprepared. For lack of preparation, King Saul failed woefully as the king of Israel. King David achieved massive success as a king because he went through a thorough preparation.

Stop waiting on God for breakthrough without working on yourself. The truth is, God is waiting on you. He has given you all that it takes in the heavens to accomplish and to complete your mission on earth. Your victory in the war is guaranteed, but you need to deploy strategies at the war front. You can do it, so do not waste this golden opportunity in the name of waiting for the right moment unprepared. There is nothing like waiting for the right moment. It will never come. Your preparation must be in consonance with your destination.

Planning is in itself a preparation process. It gives you the hope of getting out of your waiting period if it works. Knowing your destination is not a guarantee that you will get there unless you have a plan. "If I am given eight hours to chop down a tree, I will use six hours to sharpen my axe," says Abraham Lincoln. Take time to plan and commit yourself to it. Do not do what the crowd is doing.

Be Bold to Execute Your Plan

Do not just plan and expect the plan to work out by itself. You have to fight through to make your plan work out. Even your master plan may fail, but it does not mean you have failed. As you wait on the Lord and plan to take steps into your greatness, commit your ways to the Lord. Seek his counsel and approval. Make sure you do not embark on anything without His blessings. If you recognize

Him in all your doings and ascribe all the glory to Him for all the blessings He has given you, then you will go far.

If you have faith in your plan, then get to work with it. Faith without works is dead. Until you take the bull by the horns and start implementing your plan, it will remain a dead plan, and you will never see the glory of the Lord. Never be bothered about whether you will fail or not. Just take a step. God will see you through.

The only way to finish is to start.

Epilogue

*Life is not a race; it is a gift. Enjoy
it. Don't rush through it.*

At every midnight hour, my world becomes hushed. Some go to bed and enjoy their dreams. Others burn the midnight oil to consult the Supreme Being for strength, others for fresh ideas, and for some, protection. Unalike folks also call upon other beings with all sorts of motives and desires. Some also wage war on their enemies. I see new stars shine every night for the first time as newborn babes enter into this planet with new destinies. I wonder if they can walk on the right path. I again see many stars dying without shining. Some also are able to shine but are cast down before their time. I see many brilliant stars that could have shined to illuminate our world, but they leave our universe as their people kick the bucket. I lie down quietly in my room at one side of the bed gazing at the ceiling. Arms are both folded on the chest as tears water my pillow as a fountain of water falling from a mountain on opposite directions, into a river that flows to water a garden.

A few years ago, I used to stay awake in the night and ask myself questions. I used to sleep on the bare floor. In those nights, mosquitoes and cockroaches were my best friends. Used to work as an elephant but ate like an ant. At one point wished my maker made me an animal because all the arsenals of life were against me. The desire to become rich and being recognized in the society consumed me. "I have to rewrite my life story," I said to myself. An idea presented itself. My number six told me it will be delayed. *Considering my age, I have to make things happen fast lest I become old*, I thought. "Look at Paul, he is not even half your age, but his daily expenditure is more than your annual income," my mind suggested. "Because you could not afford a bottle of wine and a piece of cake on Lizzy's birthday, she left you for Alex," said my memory. My heart jumped out of my chest immediately. "I am more handsome than Alex, how can he take my Lizzy from me if not for his money? I must make money at all costs and show them that I am capable," I said. Desperation jumped in and I became perturbed. "What do I do?" I asked myself in a demoralized disposition.

Different thoughts began to flare up in my mind. On the spur of the moment, an idea walloped me. I shouted in my mind, "Eureka!" I sat up waiting for dusk to die so I could carry out my plan. I did not care about anything than being rich. I was just tired of being a mockery and mediocrity for society. No time to waste and no room for considering the end result. It would be foolish of me to die broke at age one hundred than to leave a legacy at age forty-five with fulfillment of life. At the first crow of the cock, I set off to see Baba. The moment Baba saw me, he told me not to worry, and all my heart desires will be granted. I fulfilled my requirements, and it was a brand-new day and a new song.

I was given a briefcase that is supposed to make me rich at the snap of a finger. It worked like magic. Life became so good, and I did not need God. There is no beautiful country I have not visited. Spending millions on ladies and drinks is the order of the day. My weekly *high life* expenditure alone can build a mansion. I have seen it and tasted it all. My compound is full of expensive cars. There is no enjoyment in life I have not seen. People call me the moneymaker.

What is life? Is life all about the enjoyment? Is there any kind of enjoyment or peace I can find outside what I know? If there is nothing as such, then all that I have is vanity. Today, I lie down to think of the innocent blood I have poured away. Concoctions and blood, I drink fortnightly. Now I am alone. I have no pleasure in the riches anymore. I ought to visit a public toilet to eat maggots on the last Friday of every month. I was asked to sleep with my mother who gave birth to me just to renew my covenant. My mother did not allow, and I killed her in the cause of struggle. Once in every three month, I make love to a mad woman. I have sacrificed my only brother. What kind of life have I gotten myself into? I sleep with ten different ladies every three months. Any lady I make love to either dies or suffers from an ailment that doctors cannot cure and dies eventually. Six times a year I lick the eternal sore of Baba together with other members in the fraternity for blood to ooze out, which is his blood that flows in us in covenant. Six times a year I make love to a marine spirit lady throughout the whole night.

Poor and wretched me. Who will deliver me from my hell? I have killed all my loved ones. Who am I leaving all these money and riches for? My soul was given to Satan in exchange of riches on my initiation day. Should I die tonight, I am going to hell. What profit did I get from buying cheap riches which in the end has become the most expensive that I cannot even pay for? Oh! I should have waited. I should have had patience. I should not have compared myself to Paul. I should not have gone for the cheapest way. Now I know the cheapest commodity is the most expensive of all. I cannot handle this anymore. Tonight is the last night. I will end my life. Should I get a second chance to come back on earth, I will flee evil money and devote myself to God. If you are reading my note, tell a friend to tell a friend not to do what I did. The almighty moneymaker has killed himself because he was tired of the evil life he was living. I was never happy in life, but people envied me. No one should think of taking any of the things I acquired through the pour away of innocent blood. The spirit will torment those that will take them. Bye to the world.

Never think of selling your soul to the devil for riches. Be strong and pass the test of waiting and your greatness will be peaceful. Jeremiah 17:11 says, "Like a partridge that hatches eggs it did not lay are those who gain riches by unjust means. When their lives are half gone, their riches will desert them, and in the end, they will prove to be fools." Desiring to be rich by unjust means in your waiting period will make you a fool at the end and kill you before your time. Those that sell their souls to the devil for fame and riches do not know that they are at a big loss.

The soul of a human being is priceless. It is the most expensive commodity in the entire universe. The whole resources of the earth and the entire riches of the universe cannot buy a single soul of a human being. I want to be bold to say the soul of a human being is more expensive than the blood of Jesus Christ. (I do not mean the soul of mankind is powerful than the blood of Jesus Christ, but it is more expensive than the blood.)

When God wanted to trade for the souls of mankind, He found that the only currency capable was the blood of Jesus Christ. God had the blood of Jesus Christ in His hand. He weighed the blood and the souls of mankind to establish which to go for. God became convinced that the soul of mankind is more valuable than the blood of Jesus, so he offered the blood for your soul.

In the same vein, you will only give out the money in your pocket to pick an item from the shopping mall because the item you are picking is more valuable to you than the money you are letting go. That was the kind of transaction God did.

Consider how priceless the soul is, then some people trade their souls cheaply to the devil for an amount that cannot even pay for a single hair on their head. After selling their souls, the devil then gives them hard conditions that they cannot fulfill so he can kill them and make such souls join him in hell. Do you think this is a good deal? My dear, wise up! God can bless you. If He did not withhold His only son from you, do you think it is this mere fame and riches that He cannot give to you?

What is money to God? Is he not the one that uses gold for asphalt in heaven? Just submit to him and follow His statutes. He brought you here on earth, and He holds the blueprint of your life. He can make you more than you can ever think. None of us, especially the youth, should consider choosing a path like this. Let us be willing to go through the fire today for we will shine perpetually tomorrow. There is nothing like free lunch anywhere. You may be in darkness right now but hold on. It will soon be day. Between the conception and delivery is called waiting. You need to master it. Also, remember you will have to travail like a woman in labor before your miracle will be delivered unto you.

How you carry yourself in the moment of waiting it tells when the waiting period will come to an end. It may be true you are in a challenging period of your life, but do not focus on the problem. Choose to focus on Jesus Christ—the author and the finisher of your faith. The one you fasten your eye on becomes bigger and dominates your life while the other becomes tiny and loses power in your life.

But the ship was now in the midst of the sea, tossed with waves; for the wind contrary. And in the fourth watch of the night Jesus went unto them, walking on the sea. And when the disciples saw him walking on the sea, they were troubled, saying, it is a spirit; and they cried out for fear. But straightway Jesus spoke unto them, saying, "Be of good cheer, it is I; be not afraid." And Peter answered him and said, "Lord if it be thou, bid me unto thee on the water." And he said, "Come." And when Peter was come down out of the ship, he walked on the water to go to Jesus. But when he saw the wind boisterous, he was afraid; and beginning to sink, he cried, saying, Lord, "Save me." And immediately Jesus stretched forth his hand and caught him and said unto him,

"O thou of little faith, wherefore didst thou doubt?" (Matthew 14:24–31)

The disciples of Jesus were in the middle of the sea. The raging sea scared them to death. They believed that all hope of survival was gone due to the state they found themselves. In the middle of the storm, Jesus appeared on the scene walking on the sea. The first message Jesus gave them was to be of good cheer. Although, they were perishing, but the message to them from the son of God was for them to be of good cheer. Why? Because he was still with them. Irrespective of your war in life, be of good cheer for Jesus Christ is with you. You are not alone. The storms you see today, you shall conquer only if you will not be of little faith and doubt as Peter did.

Peter told Jesus that, "If it is you Lord, ask me to come to you on the water." Jesus asked him to come. Peter jumped onto the sea, and he did not sink. He had his eyes fixed on Jesus, and he began to walk to Jesus' direction. The moment Peter took his eyes off Jesus and considered the raging sea, he began to sink so fast.

If you will take your eyes and attention off the situation and focus on Jesus and believe in Him, you will walk on your sea and you shall not drown. The time Peter was walking on the sea with his eyes focused on Jesus, the storm was still blowing in fury, but he never felt it. Little did he know that he was the same person that cried out of fear that he was perishing. The time he was looking unto Jesus, he forgot his problems. He was able to do the impossible by walking on the sea in the middle of the storm.

You have been so mindful of your problems for far too long. Choose to forget about it this day and look unto Jesus for once and you will see the difference. The other day, the Psalmist said, "He will lift up his eyes to the hills." From whence cometh his help. His help cometh from the Lord. The Lord who made the heavens and earth. Your help comes from the Lord. Learn to depend on him. Choose to look unto him only and always.

The Lord will make you like a cornerstone. The builders can reject a cornerstone during the foundation of a building, but they will definitely look for it before the building can be completed. Your success may be like a Chinese bamboo tree. Keep watering it. If you stop watering it, it will die in the ground. The day it sprouts out, it will run faster than those that germinated earlier. Remember, the taller and mightier your building, the deeper your foundation. Take time to lay a good foundation.

You will not fail in life if you do not want to. Tell yourself you got this fight, and you will never surrender just as you cannot retreat. Fight and fight hard. If you have not seen a Hollywood movie entitled *Creed*, I encourage you to find it and watch over and again. Fight like the character of Adonis Creed in the movie if you want to be a champion in life. This movie will teach you preparation, determination, and zeal. Again, if you have not seen the movie entitled *Acrimony*, I encourage you to watch it too. It will teach you the necessity for endurance and perseverance. Never aspire to be inspired by cheap glory. They do not last for long, and their ends are disgraced.

I hope to see you at the top. God bless you.

Don't rush the process. Good things take time.

About the Author

Newton Duah Yeboah is a student of the Word of God. He is an accountant by profession, a husband, a father, and inspirational speaker. Newton believes every individual is a gift from God unto humanity. He believes we are all unique in our various capacities, and with the right attitude and help, no one will fail in life. It is his vision to bring smile, hope, comfort, and the peace of God to as many as he will be able to touch. He also believes every vision is probable with God.

www.ingramcontent.com/pod-product-compliance
Lightning Source LLC
Chambersburg PA
CBHW020602160726
47991CB00002B/835